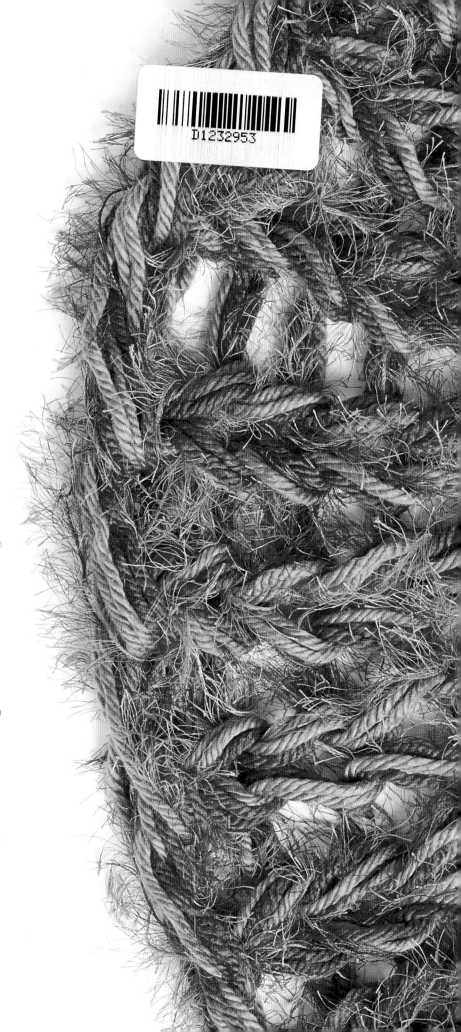

First published in this format 2014

Text and Patterns: Linda Zemba Burhance
Jacket/Cover and Interior Design: Kimberly Adis
Photographer: Alexandra Grablewski
Executive Editor, Series: Shawna Mullen
Assistant Editor, Series: Timothy Stobierski
Series Art Director: Rosalind Loeb Wanke
Series Production Editor: Lynne Phillips
Series Copy Editor: Diane Sinitsky

 The Taunton Press
Inspiration for hands-on living®

The Taunton Press, Inc., 63 South Main Street,
PO Box 5506, Newtown, CT 06470-5506
e-mail: tp@taunton.com

Threads® is a trademark of The Taunton Press,
Inc., registered in the U.S. Patent and
Trademark Office.

The following names/manufacturers appearing
in *Fashionista Arm Knitting* are trademarks:
Lion Brand® Chenille™; Lion Brand Fun Fur®;
Lion Brand Hometown USA®; Loops & Threads®
Poodle™; Martha Stewart Crafts™; Premier®
Yarns Starbella®; Red Heart® Boutique
Sassy Fabric™

Library of Congress Cataloging-in-Publication
Data

Burhance, Linda Zemba.
  Fashionista arm knitting : luxe wraps, tops,
cowls, and other no-needle knits / Linda Zemba
Burhance.
     pages cm
  ISBN 978-1-62710-956-7
  1. Shawls. 2. Knitwear. 3. Finger weaving. 4.
Knitting--Patterns. I. Title.
  TT825.B866 2014
  746.43'2--dc23
                              2014025472

Printed in the United States of America
10 9 8 7 6 5 4 3 2 1

CONTENTS

20
WRAP ME IN
LUXURY

22
LOOP D LOOP

24
FLAME THROWER

26
TIE ONE ON

28
SHADES OF GRAY

INTRODUCTION

Arm knitting is so much fun! And the best part is you can do it, even if you don't know how to knit!

SOMEONE SAID TO ME THAT WHEN I arm knit, it is like my arms are dancing—I couldn't agree more! This booklet is dedicated to all of the fashionistas out there who love fashion and love to create. Recently, I was at a major fashion show in New York City, where I was inspired by all of the textiles and textures. Chunky knits and high textures are huge among high-end designers right now, and you can create these off-the-runway looks yourself for a fraction of the cost. I hope you'll find this booklet inspirational and a starting point to making a look all your own.

Let's talk about sizing. Arm knitting is a very flexible form of knitting. Everyone's arms are different, so I have given you a general measurement guideline to go by. If you need to adjust the length or width, no worries; you can easily add an extra couple of stitches or rows to accommodate your own shape. All measurements are taken on a flat surface because arm knitting is so loose that the moment gravity is involved, it stretches. You can work with this drapability to create beautiful, fluid garments. The patterns provided here give you a one-size-fits-*most* starting point, but it's easy to create a size that fits.

A note about notions: I suggest having a flexible tape measure, scissors, and some needle and thread on hand for these projects. One project specifically calls for a "stitch holder," which is a knitting tool that is usually available wherever you buy yarn. A crochet hook can be used to connect the garments together, but I prefer to use my hands. I also have been known to use a couple of potato-chip-bag clips (the ones without teeth) to hold the garment pieces together as I weave in the ends. Necessity is the mother of invention, as they say!

Because arm knitting is so loose, the ends tend to work their way back out over time. To prevent this, use a needle and thread to hand-stitch the ends in place once they are woven into the work. This is especially important for garments; you wouldn't want a shoulder or side seam to unravel when you're out walking or dancing! Taking those extra few minutes after finishing your project to stitch everything in place will save you a lot of repair time down the road, so I strongly encourage it for each of the projects in this booklet.

CASTING ON

This type of casting on is called a **Long Tail Cast On**. Arm knitting always involves using multiple strands of yarn at once. Here I am using six strands of yarn, but you will use however many strands are specified in your project.

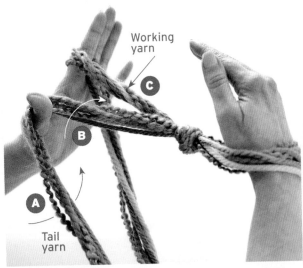

1. Make a slip knot and put it on your right hand. Wrap the working yarn (yarn coming off of the skein) around your pointer finger, and the tail yarn (yarn closest to your body) around your thumb as shown. With your right hand, go under the tail yarn **(A)**, over strands **(B)**, and grasp the working yarn **(C)**.

2. Pull the yarn that you've just grasped up to make a loop. Then let go with your left hand.

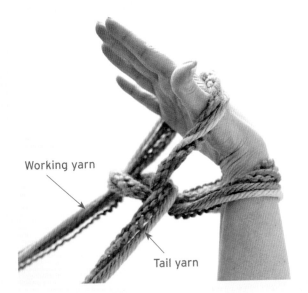

3. Put the newly created loop (stitch) onto your right hand. Lightly tighten, but be sure that the stitch is not too tight.

4. You now have two stitches cast on. Repeat steps 1 through 3, creating stitches on your right hand until you have the number of stitches called for in your pattern.

ARM KNITTING

As Easy as One, Two, Three!

1. Hold the working yarn in your right hand. Grasp a stitch in your left hand.

2. Pull the stitch over your working yarn.

3. Place the new stitch on the left arm, and repeat until all stitches are on your left arm.

Now Go Back the Other Way!

4. Hold the working yarn in your left hand. Grasp a stitch in your right hand.

5. Pull the stitch over your working yarn.

6. Place the new stitch on the right arm, and repeat until all stitches are on your right arm.

KNIT TWO TOGETHER

"Knitting two stitches together" (K2tog in knitting lingo) removes a stitch from your row, making it great for projects that need to angle. Just hold two stitches together and pull the working yarn through both stitches at the same time as if they are a single stitch to achieve the effect. **"Slip, slip, knit"** (SSK) is used to create the mirror image of K2tog. Just slip two stitches onto your opposite hand, and use the working yarn to knit the two stitches together by pulling the working yarn through the two stitches at the same time. Use K2tog and SSK on opposite sides of a garment to create a beautiful angled effect.

CASTING OFF

For all of these projects, you will always end your knitting with the stitches on your left arm. Now, you are ready to finish your project by casting off. Here's how.

1. Knit two stitches onto your right hand.

2. Pull the first stitch over the second stitch and let go. Your stitches should remain fairly loose.

3. Keep knitting one stitch at a time and pulling the previous stitch over the one you just knit until you have none left. It's super easy!

4. Now that you've completed your work, all you have to do is weave your ends in and you are done!

fashionista
TIP

For more glamour, add
some sparkly buttons
or sew on a rhinestone
or two.

HALF-AND-HALF
MIXED-MEDIA COWL

SKILL LEVEL
Intermediate

MEASUREMENTS
32" long (before connecting)

10" wide

YARN
2 skeins super bulky roving-like yarn (CYCA 6)–YARN A

Prewound Ball:

1 skein eyelash-type bulky yarn (CYCA 5)–YARN B

1 skein super bulky yarn (CYCA 6)–YARN C

SHOWN IN
Lion Brand® Imagine super bulky yarn (CYCA 6) in Blueberry Hill–YARN A

Lion Brand Fun Fur® eyelash-type bulky yarn (CYCA 5) in Aquamarine–YARN B

Lion Brand Hometown USA® super bulky yarn (CYCA 6) in Fort Worth Blue–YARN C

NOTIONS
Needle and thread

To Make the Cowl

1. Make sure to read the Knitting Notes below to make your prewound ball before you begin. Then, using the first skein of YARN A, cast on 6 stitches, leaving a 12" tail, as shown on p. 5.

2. Knit 3 rows, as shown on p. 6. Do not cast off. For your next row, pick up the prewound ball containing three strands of YARN B and three strands of YARN C. Holding the six strands of the prewound ball together, tie onto the tail of YARN A for stability while knitting. Knit 6 stitches across YARN A, using your prewound ball yarns. Knit 8 more rows from the prewound ball. Do not cast off. To complete, use your second skein of YARN A, tying YARN A onto the tails of the prewound ball at the first stitch for stability, and knit 3 more rows for a total length of 32".

3. Cast off, as shown on p. 7, leaving an approximately 24" tail to connect the cowl.

Finishing

Place the work on a flat surface, and position the short end of the YARN A section to the long side of the YARN A section. Weave the YARN A tail back and forth to connect. Tie in any remaining loose ends.

KNITTING NOTES Before you start arm knitting this project, you need to make a prewound ball that combines three strands of YARN B and three strands of YARN C. Here is how: Measure off three separate 10-yard lengths of YARN B and three separate 10-yard lengths of YARN C. Grasp all six strands together, and wind into one big ball. Set aside for later. This is your prewound ball.

IT'S ALL BLACK AND WHITE TO ME
VELVETY CROP TOP

SKILL LEVEL
Beginner

MEASUREMENTS
20" long
20" wide

YARN
2 skeins bulky yarn
(CYCA 5)—YARN A

4 skeins super bulky yarn
(CYCA 6)—YARN B

SHOWN IN
Lion Brand Velvet Spun
bulky yarn (CYCA 5) in
White—YARN A

Loops & Threads® Radiant
super bulky yarn (CYCA 6)
in Safari—YARN B

NOTIONS
Needle and thread to
stabilize yarn ends

To Make the Garment

1. Holding three strands together (one strand of YARN A and two strands of YARN B), cast on 8 stitches, as shown on p. 5, leaving an 18" tail.

2. Knit each row, as shown on p. 6. Continue the process until you reach your desired length of approximately 9 rows or 20".

3. Cast off, as shown on p. 7, leaving an approximately 18" tail. This finished piece is the front of the garment. Make the back of the garment in the same way.

Finishing

Lay the front panel on top of the back panel, with wrong sides together. Using your yarn tail, tie the panels together at the hem. Weave back and forth, connecting the front to the back at the sides for approximately 3 rows. At the top of the work, use the cast-off tail to weave back and forth between the front and the back approximately 3 stitches from each side, leaving the neck opening.

KNITTING NOTES I have called for an extra skein of YARN A due to the yardage amount listed on the skein. You will have some of this yarn left over, which is better than running out. You can use the leftover yarn in another project, such as a scarf.

JEWEL OF THE NIGHT
VARIEGATED RIBBON TOP

SKILL LEVEL
Beginner

MEASUREMENTS
20" long
20" wide

YARN
5 skeins ribbon-type super bulky yarn (CYCA 6)

SHOWN IN
Premier® Yarns Starbella® ribbon-type super bulky yarn (CYCA 6) in Canyon Sunrise

NOTIONS
Needle and thread to stabilize yarn ends

To Make the Garment

1. Holding two strands of the yarn together, cast on 12 stitches, as shown on p. 5.

2. Knit each row, as shown on p. 6. Continue the process until you reach your desired length of approximately 9 rows or 20".

3. Cast off, as shown on p. 7. This is the front panel of your garment. Make the back panel in the same way.

Finishing

Lay the front panel on top of the back panel with wrong sides together. Using your yarn tails, tie the front panel to the back panel at the hem. Weave the ends back and forth, connecting sides, for approximately 4 rows or 6". At the top of the work, use the tail to attach the shoulders by weaving back and forth for approximately 4 stitches from the edge, leaving the neck opening. Take care in this step so that your seams look pretty because they are so visible. Use a needle and thread to stabilize the ends of the yarn.

KNITTING NOTES There are several types of ribbon yarns on the market. Some of them unravel easily, so I suggest handling with care when knitting. Remove all jewelry, and definitely take the time at the end of the project to stitch the ends of the yarn in place. Turn the ends of the yarn a couple of times to hide the raw edges, and make tiny hand stitches in a similar thread color to stabilize. You'll be glad you did!

GLITTER AND GLAM
SHAGGY RIBBON SHRUG

SKILL LEVEL
Intermediate

MEASUREMENTS
72" long (before connecting into shrug)
6" wide

YARN
3 skeins ribbon-type bulky yarn (CYCA 5)—YARN A

3 skeins fur-type super bulky yarn (CYCA 6)—YARN B

SHOWN IN
Lion Brand Martha Stewart Crafts™ Glitter Ribbon bulky yarn (CYCA 5) in Garnet—YARN A

Lion Brand Romance fur-type super bulky yarn (CYCA 6) in Lipstick—YARN B

NOTIONS
Needle and thread to stabilize yarn ends

To Make the Garment

1. Holding three strands of YARN A and three strands of YARN B together, cast on 6 stitches, leaving a 36" tail, as shown on p. 5.

2. Knit approximately 27 rows or 72" from the bottom of the work.

3. Cast off, leaving a 36" tail, as shown on p. 7.

Finishing

Lay your knitted rectangle on a flat surface. Shape the work into an oval on the table, with the short sides of the work touching. Weave in the yarn tails to connect the short sides together. Mark the center of the inside of the oval with a safety pin, directly above the seam you just made. Use the pin to connect the inside center of the oval together. It will look almost like a sideways figure 8 with two openings on either side of the pin for your armholes. Then, with a length of yarn, weave together a few stitches on either side of the pin, connecting the upper and lower center of the oval, creating the center-back seam of the shrug. Tie off the yarn ends, and sew with a needle and thread. Take care in this step to ensure that your top is secure.

KNITTING NOTES It is important to secure the fur and ribbon yarns when you are finished creating your garment. These types of yarns are very slippery and can easily unravel in the loose knit that arm knitting creates. I believe the best strategy is sewing the ribbon and fur yarn back to itself after tying it into a loose knot. You can use a sewing machine if you are comfortable with that, or just hand-stitch the yarns in place with a needle and thread using a similar color thread on the wrong side of the work.

fashionista
TIP

Wear this over your
favorite little black
dress! Can you say
fashionista?

NICE ICE, BABY
PEPLUM SWING TOP

SKILL LEVEL
Intermediate

MEASUREMENTS
18" long at center back
18" wide across chest

YARN
6 skeins bulky yarn
(CYCA 5)

SHOWN IN
Lion Brand Chenille™ bulky
yarn (CYCA 5) in Granite

NOTIONS
Needle and thread to
stabilize yarn ends

To Make the Garment

1. Holding six strands of the yarn together at the same time, cast on 20 stitches, as shown on p. 5, leaving a 36" tail.

2. Knit 1 row, as shown on p. 6. For the next row, K2tog, as shown on p. 7, all the way across the row. You now have 10 stitches. Next, knit across 10 stitches for 7 rows or approximately 18" from the bottom of the work.

3. Cast off, as shown on p. 7, leaving a 36" tail. This is the front panel of your garment. Make the back panel in the same way.

Finishing

Lay the front panel on top of the back panel with wrong sides together. Using your yarn tails, tie the front panel to the back panel at the hem. Weave in the tail to connect the sides approximately 4 rows or 6" up. At the top of the work, use the tail to attach at the shoulders, weaving in to connect the shoulders approximately 2 stitches in from each edge, which will leave a neck opening.

KNITTING NOTES It is important to secure the yarn ends of the work because of the large stitches created in this arm-knitting pattern. The best way to secure the yarn is with a sewing needle and thread in the same color as the yarn, on the inside of the garment. Just remember to keep the yarn as loose as the stitches! I suggest putting it on a flat surface inside out to determine where the best place is to stabilize the yarn ends, making sure to include all six strands.

fashionista
TIP

Try wearing this top
over a T-shirt dress,
and add fun legwear
for on-trend style.

fashionista
TIP

Wear this top over a pair
of black leggings and fun
boots to show off your
passion for fashion.

AMETHYST ALLURE
TUNIC WITH COWL NECK

SKILL LEVEL
Intermediate

MEASUREMENTS
27" long at center back
18" wide across chest

YARN
9 skeins bulky yarn
(CYCA 5)

SHOWN IN
Lion Brand Chenille bulky
yarn (CYCA 5) in Amethyst

NOTIONS
Needle and thread to
stabilize yarn ends

To Make the Garment

1. Holding six strands of the yarn together, cast on 20 stitches, as shown on p. 5, leaving a 36" tail.

2. Knit 1 row, as shown on p. 6. For the next row, K2tog, as shown on p. 7, all the way across the row. You now have 10 stitches. For the next row, knit across 10 stitches for 9 rows or approximately 26" from the bottom of the work on a flat surface.

3. Cast off, as shown on p. 7. This is the front panel of your garment. Make the back panel in the same way.

4. To make the cowl: Holding six strands of the yarn together, cast on 8 stitches, leaving a 36" tail. Knit 5 rows or approximately 12", as shown on p. 6. Leave a 36" tail. Cast off, as shown on p. 7.

Finishing

Lay your front panel on top of the back panel with wrong sides together. Using your yarn tails, tie the front panel to the back panel at the hem. Weave the tail back and forth to connect the sides for approximately 6 rows or 12" up from the hem. At the top of the work, use the tail to attach the front to the back at the shoulders, weaving back and forth to connect for approximately 2 stitches in from the edge, leaving the neck opening. Attach the cowl by placing the short sides of the rectangle together and weaving the yarn tail up the short side. Place the cowl onto the neck opening of the tunic, and weave the tail back and forth to connect. Tie off the ends. Take care in this step to ensure that your top is secure.

KNITTING NOTES Because of the length and the amount of yarn, my suggestion is to work over a table to support the garment. When finished knitting, use a needle and thread to sew the yarn back to itself to prevent unraveling.

fashionista
TIP

This collared cape can go from day (over your coat) to night (over your gown). You are the star of the show in this look!

WRAP ME IN LUXURY
DOUBLE COLLARED CAPELET

SKILL LEVEL
Intermediate

MEASUREMENTS
12" long before connecting ends
32" wide

YARN
4 skeins super bulky yarn
(CYCA 6)—YARN A, YARN B
2 skeins eyelash-type bulky yarn
(CYCA 5)—YARN C, YARN D

SHOWN IN
Lion Brand Hometown USA super
bulky yarn (CYCA 6) in Honolulu
Pink—YARN A and New Orleans
French Berry—YARN B

Lion Brand Fun Fur eyelash-
type bulky yarn (CYCA 5)
in Raspberry—YARN C and
Flamingo—YARN D

NOTIONS
Needle and thread to
stabilize yarn ends

To Make the Garment

1. Hold together two strands each of YARN A and YARN B
and one strand each of YARN C and YARN D (for a total of
six strands), and cast on 15 stitches, as shown on p. 5.

2. Knit each row, as shown on p. 6. Continue the process until
you reach your desired length of approximately 5 rows or 12".

3. Cast off, as shown on p. 7 This is the first panel of your
garment. Make the second panel in the same way.

Finishing

Lay one panel on top of the other with right sides together
on a flat surface. Grasping the first and last stitches of the
cast-off edge of each side, bring together in a circle, slightly
overlapping the first and last stitch. Using your cast-off tails,
weave them back and forth to connect the collar to the cape
at the cast-off edges. Tie off the ends. Weave in the remaining
yarn tails from the cast-on edges. Tie off.

KNITTING NOTES I found it helpful to use potato-chip-bag clips to hold the two
rectangles in place while connecting them. Just be sure to use clips without teeth;
you don't want to snag your work!

LOOP D LOOP
POODLE BOLERO VEST

SKILL LEVEL
Advanced

MEASUREMENTS
15" long at center back

21" wide at bottom back hem

YARN
8 skeins loopy-type super bulky yarn (CYCA 6)

SHOWN IN
Loops & Threads Poodle™ loopy-type super bulky yarn (CYCA 6) in Black

NOTIONS
Needle and thread to stabilize yarn ends

To Make the Back

1. Holding together four strands of yarn, cast on 8 stitches, as shown on p. 5, leaving a 36" tail. Knit 2 rows, as shown on p. 6.

2. For the next row, K2tog, as shown on p. 7; knit 4 stitches; K2tog. You now have 6 stitches. Knit 2 rows. Cast off all 6 stitches, as shown on p. 7.

To Make the Left Front

1. Holding together four strands of yarn, cast on 6 stitches, leaving a 36" tail. Knit 2 rows.

2. K2tog and then knit 4. You now have 5 stitches. Knit 1 row. K2tog and then knit 3. You now have 4 stitches. Cast off these remaining 4 stitches.

To Make the Right Front

1. Holding together four strands of yarn, cast on 6 stitches, leaving a 36" tail. Knit 2 rows.

2. Next row, knit 4, then K2tog. You now have 5 stitches. Knit 1 row. Knit 3, then K2tog. You now have 4 stitches. Cast off remaining 4 stitches.

Finishing

Lay the left front and right front panels on top of the back panel, with wrong sides together. Using your yarn tails, join the front panel to the back panel at the sides. Tie off. Then, using your cast-off tails, weave the tail back and forth to connect the shoulders 4 stitches in on each side. You will have 2 unconnected stitches in the center of the back piece for the back neck opening.

KNITTING NOTES This yarn makes it hard for others to spot flaws (always a plus!), but it is also easy to drop a strand because of its loopy construction. Make sure you are using all four strands in every stitch. If the decreasing intimidates you, just make a giant boa by casting on 6 stitches and knitting back and forth until the yarn is almost gone, leaving enough to cast off. It's just as glamorous and super easy!

FLAME THROWER
STRIPED TOP

SKILL LEVEL
Intermediate

MEASUREMENTS
18" long
16" wide

YARN
3 skeins eyelash-type bulky yarn (CYCA 5)—YARN A, YARN B, YARN C

3 skeins super bulky yarn (CYCA 6)—YARN D, YARN E, YARN F

SHOWN IN
Lion Brand Fun Fur eyelash-type bulky yarn (CYCA 5) in Neon Orange—YARN A, Raspberry—YARN B, and Flamingo—YARN C

Lion Brand Hometown USA super bulky yarn (CYCA 6) in Neon Orange—YARN D, Honolulu Pink—YARN E, and New Orleans French Berry—YARN F

NOTIONS
Needle and thread to stabilize yarn ends

To Make the Garment

1. Make Stripe 1 (see Knitting Notes below) by casting on 12 stitches, as shown on p. 5, leaving a 72" tail to sew the garment together at the end of the project. For the next row, make Stripe 2 by knitting 1 row. Make sure you tie the Stripe 2 yarns onto the first stitch to keep from unraveling. This is a very loose and open knit that will need a lot of stability even while you are knitting. For the next row, make Stripe 3 by knitting 1 row, making sure to tie the new color on as you did for Stripe 2.

2. Knit approximately 9 more rows or 18", alternating between Stripes 1, 2, and 3 in order, until you reach your desired length.

3. Cast off, as shown on p. 7, using the Stripe 3 yarn combination. This is the front panel of your garment. Make the back panel in the same way.

Finishing

Gently place the front panel on top of the back panel with wrong sides together, lining up the stripes. This is a delicate knit, so be careful not to pull the stitches when positioning. Using your yarn tail, tie the front panel to the back panel at the hem. Weave the ends in *very* loosely, taking care not to pull stitches, for approximately 8 rows or 14". At the top of the work, use your cast-off yarn tail to attach at the shoulders, weaving in ends approximately 3 stitches from the edge, leaving the neck opening.

KNITTING NOTES To create the stripe pattern: • Stripe 1: Hold together one strand each of YARNS A and D • Stripe 2: Hold together one strand each of YARNS B and E • Stripe 3: Hold together one strand each of YARNS C and F

fashionista
TIP

Keep knitting until the
garment hits the floor
for an over-the-top
fashion look. (Just make
sure to buy more yarn!)

TIE ONE ON
TIE-ON INFINITY SCARF

SKILL LEVEL
Beginner

MEASUREMENTS
56" long (flat on table)
6" wide (flat on table)

YARN
1 skein eyelash-type bulky yarn (CYCA 5)

1 card fabric-strip bulky yarn (CYCA 6)

(Note: You can use any precut fabric strip approximately 2½" wide by 30 yards long)

SHOWN IN
Lion Brand Fun Fur eyelash-type bulky yarn (CYCA 5) in Raspberry

Red Heart® Boutique Sassy Fabric™ super bulky (CYCA 6) in Pink Dot

To Make the Garment

1. Holding one strand of Fun Fur and one strand of Sassy Fabric together, cast on 5 stitches, as shown on p. 5, leaving an 18" length of tail yarns to use to tie the garment on at the end of the project.

2. Knit each row, as shown on p. 6, for approximately 29 rows or 52".

3. Cast off, as shown on p. 7, leaving an 18" tail to use to tie on the scarf.

Finishing

Wrap the scarf twice around your neck, and use your yarn tails to tie into a bow.

KNITTING NOTES Eyelash yarn makes a huge impact on this project. Because it is so tiny, it is easy to drop the eyelash yarn strands as you knit, so be conscious of this as you go. For double the impact, add another skein of eyelash and see what happens! With arm knitting, you can take chances with creativity.

SHADES OF GRAY
SLEEVELESS TURTLENECK

SKILL LEVEL
Advanced

MEASUREMENTS
29" long from top of cowl to hem

18" wide before shoulder decreases

YARN
4 skeins total super bulky yarn (CYCA 6)—YARN A (1 skein), YARN B (3 skeins)

SHOWN IN
Lion Brand Hometown USA super bulky yarn (CYCA 6) in Kansas City Wheat—YARN A and Charcoal—YARN B

NOTIONS
Stitch holder

Needle and thread to stabilize yarn ends

To Make the Garment

1. Holding two strands of YARN A together at the same time (see Knitting Notes below), cast on 20 stitches, as shown on p. 5. Knit 2 rows. Remove the work from your arm by placing it onto a stitch holder. Turn the work around to the opposite side (purl side), and remove from the stitch holder by placing it back on the *same arm* so that the purl side is now facing you.

2. Pick up two strands of YARN B, and tie onto the first stitch to prevent unraveling. Using two strands of YARN B, knit 1 row across, as shown on p. 6. For the next row, K2Tog, as shown on p. 7, all the way across the row. You now have 10 stitches. For the next row, knit across 10 stitches for 7 rows.

3. Shoulder decreases: For the next row, SSK, as shown on p. 7; knit 6 across; K2tog. Then knit 1 row. For the next row, SSK, knit 4 across, K2tog. Do not cast off.

continued on p. 30

KNITTING NOTES Instead of buying extra balls of yarn, you can do prep work to set yourself up with a double-strand ball made out of one skein. Just divide a skein of YARN A into two balls, then rewind into one ball of double-strand yarn. Repeat with a single skein of YARN B. If you are not comfortable doing this, just buy one skein extra of each color to knit with double strands, and use leftover yarn to make a belt for an extra fashion punch—3 stitches by 40 rows is all it takes!

4. Turtleneck: Knit back and forth for 5 rows and then cast off, as shown on p. 7. This is the front panel of your garment. Make the back panel of your garment in the same way.

Finishing

Lay your front panel on top of the back panel with wrong sides together. Using your yarn tails, tie the front panel to the back panel at the hem, connecting contrast hem color YARN A first. Then, using a double-strand length YARN B, weave back and forth, connecting the sides for approximately 7 rows or 12" up from the hem. Next, using a double-strand length of YARN B, weave back and forth, connecting the sides of the turtleneck. I highly recommend using a needle and thread to stabilize the ends of the yarn to themselves because this is such a loose knit and tying off the yarn will be visible.

Look for these other *Threads* Selects booklets at www.tauntonstore.com and wherever crafts are sold.

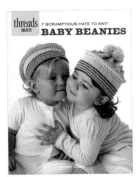

Baby Beanies
Debby Ware

EAN: 9781621137634
8½ x 10⅞, 32 pages
Product# 078001
$9.95 U.S., $9.95 Can.

Cute Pets to Knit
Susie Johns

EAN: 9781627107747
8½ x 10⅞, 32 pages
Product# 078043
$9.95 U.S., $9.95 Can.

Pet Projects to Knit
Sally Muir and Joanna Osborne

EAN: 9781627100991
8½ x 10⅞, 32 pages
Product# 078034
$9.95 U.S., $9.95 Can.

Dog Coats & Collars
Sally Muir and Joanna Osborne

EAN: 9781627100984
8½ x 10⅞, 32 pages
Product# 078033
$9.95 U.S., $9.95 Can.

Socktopus Socks
Alice Yu

EAN: 9781627101004
8½ x 10⅞, 32 pages
Product# 078035
$9.95 U.S., $9.95 Can.

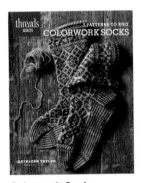

Colorwork Socks
Kathleen Taylor

EAN: 9781621137740
8½ x 10⅞, 32 pages
Product# 078011
$9.95 U.S., $9.95 Can.

Fair Isle Flower Garden
Kathleen Taylor

EAN: 9781621137702
8½ x 10⅞, 32 pages
Product# 078008
$9.95 U.S., $9.95 Can.

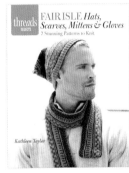

Fair Isle Hats, Scarves, Mittens & Gloves
Kathleen Taylor

EAN: 9781621137719
8½ x 10⅞, 32 pages
Product# 078009
$9.95 U.S., $9.95 Can.

Felted Scarves, Hats & Mittens
Kathleen Taylor

EAN: 9781627100960
8½ x 10⅞, 32 pages
Product # 078031
$9.95 U.S., $9.95 Can.

Favorite Felted Gifts to Knit
Kathleen Taylor

EAN: 9781627101653
8½ x 10⅞, 32 pages
Product# 078038
$9.95 U.S., $9.95 Can.

Shawlettes
Jean Moss

EAN: 9781621137726
8½ x 10⅞, 32 pages
Product# 078010
$9.95 U.S., $9.95 Can.

Cable Shawlettes
Jean Moss

EAN: 9781621137733
8½ x 10⅞, 32 pages
Product# 078037
$9.95 U.S., $9.95 Can.

If you like these projects, you'll love these other fun craft booklets

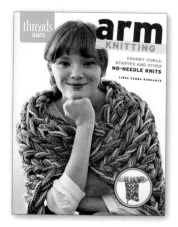

Arm Knitting
Chunky cowls, scarves, and other no-needle knits
Linda Zemba Burhance

Knitting your own scarf, cowl, or blanket is easier than you think, and with the brilliant new technique called arm knitting, it couldn't be quicker. Each of these 12 projects knit up in under an hour and only require a few skeins of yarn. Best of all, you don't need any tools—just bring your arms and hands! Go wild with the bright colors of the Fun Times Scarf, add a sophisticated layer to your date-night outfit with the Evening Sparkle Tie-on Shrug, or just cuddle up with the Super Cozy Throw. Just know that your friends are going to want some of their own!

32 pages, product #078045, $9.95 U.S.

Bungee Band Bracelets & More
12 projects to make with bungee band & paracord
Vera Vandenbosch

Bungee cord is no longer just a tool—now available in a wide variety of colors and thicknesses, it's the perfect material for you to create beautiful bracelets and necklaces. The 12 projects in this booklet will show you exactly how to transform this stretchy material into runway-worthy designs for you to wear and show off.

32 pages, product #078048, $9.95 U.S.

DecoDen Bling
Mini decorations for phones & favorite things
Alice Fisher

DecoDen is all about bringing bling to every aspect of your life—from your sunglasses to your cellphone to everything in between! Best of all, the decadent sparkle of this hot decorating style is just a few simple techniques away. From phone cases to wall clocks to picture frames and more, the 20 recipes in this booklet will show you exactly what you need to glam up your day.

32 pages, product #078046, $9.95 U.S.